PIANO • VOCAL • GUITAR

BILLY JOEL

THE NYLON CURTAIN

T0084083

Additional editing and transcription by David Rosenthal

ISBN 978-1-5400-8311-1

HAL • LEONARD®

Visit Hal Leonard Online at
www.halleonard.com

Contact us:
Hal Leonard
7777 West Bluemound Road
Milwaukee, WI 53213
Email: info@halleonard.com

In Europe, contact:
Hal Leonard Europe Limited
42 Wigmore Street
Marylebone, London, W1U 2RN
Email: info@halleonardeurope.com

In Australia, contact:
Hal Leonard Australia Pty. Ltd.
4 Lentara Court
Cheltenham, Victoria, 3192 Australia
Email: info@halleonard.com.au

FOREWORD

Released in 1982, *The Nylon Curtain* was Billy Joel's eighth studio album and the fourth to be produced by Phil Ramone. It was one of the first albums ever to be digitally recorded, mixed, and mastered. The album peaked at number seven on the *Billboard* charts and yielded two top 20 singles, "Allentown" and "Pressure."

Billy set out to create a masterpiece like The Beatles' *Sgt. Pepper*, crafting the songs in the studio during the recording process and "playing" the studio as though it were another instrument in the band. It took a long time to record, but to this day Billy says *The Nylon Curtain* is "the recording I'm most proud of and the material I'm most proud of."

Lyrically he dove deep into many of the topics of the day—from the soldier's point of view during the Vietnam War ("Goodnight Saigon"), to America's declining steel industry ("Allentown"), to dealing with the stresses of life ("Pressure"). Musically he took chances with adventurous chord changes, such as in "Laura" and "Surprises," and the entire work is conceptually "bookended" when the main melody of the first track "Allentown" returns at the end of the album during the fade out of "Where's the Orchestra."

Having played keyboards in Billy Joel's band since 1993, I have an inside perspective into his music. Accordingly, Billy asked that I review every note of the sheet music in his entire catalog of songs. As a pianist, he entrusted me with the task of correcting and re-transcribing each piece to ensure that the printed music represents each song exactly as it was written and recorded. This is the latest edition in our series of revised songbooks in the Billy Joel catalog.

The challenge with each folio in Billy's catalog is to find musical ways to combine his piano parts and vocal melodies into playable piano arrangements. First, the signature piano parts are transcribed and notated exactly as Billy played them. The vocal melodies are then transcribed and incorporated into the piano part in a way that preserves the original character of each song. Billy's piano embellishments between his vocal phrases are also included wherever they're playable along with the vocal melodies.

The ascending thematic intro of "Goodnight Saigon" is played many times throughout the song. However, each time it is slightly different depending on which part of the song it transitions to. The subtle variations of this theme are critical in tying together the different sections of the song, so each of these piano parts is transcribed exactly.

The chromatic, almost atonal themes of "Scandinavian Skies" push the limits of tonality while supporting the mood of the lyrics. These themes, played by a string quartet, are transcribed exactly. The rhythm of the string quartet in the choruses is quite tricky to play at the same time as the melody, so I simplified it a bit to make it more playable. However, the actual rhythm that's on the record is shown as an *ossia* part at the bottom of the page.

On "She's Right on Time," the three-part vocal harmonies in the chorus are an important part of the character of the song, so they are written into the piano part. The vocal harmonies are also shown on an additional vocal staff as cue notes, so that the lead vocal melody can be shown on its own staff.

The piano voicings in "Where's the Orchestra" are written as close as possible to the record while still being able to be played simultaneously with the vocal melody. On the record, the song fades out during the reprise of the "Allentown" theme, so I included the ending that we play when we perform it live.

All of the songs in this collection received the same astute attention to detail. The result is sheet music that is both accurate and enjoyable to play, and that remains true to the original performances.

Billy and I are pleased to present the revised and now accurate sheet music to the classic album *The Nylon Curtain*.

Enjoy,

David Rosenthal
May 2021

CONTENTS

ALLENTOWN

Words and Music by
BILLY JOEL

LAURA

Words and Music by
BILLY JOEL

PRESSURE

Words and Music by
BILLY JOEL

You have __ to learn __ to pace __ your - self. __
You used __ to call __ me par - a - noid. __
Don't ask __ for help; __ you're all __ a - lone. __

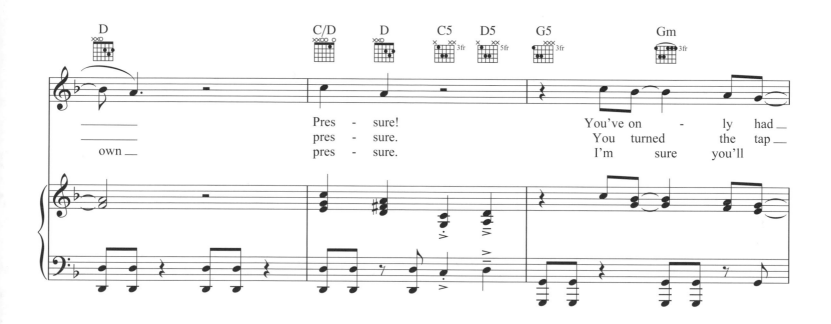

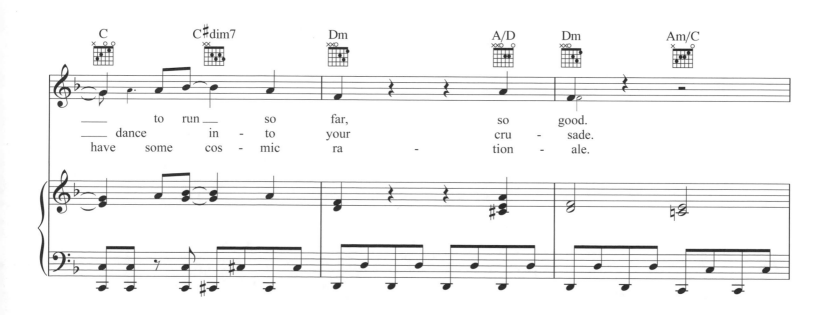

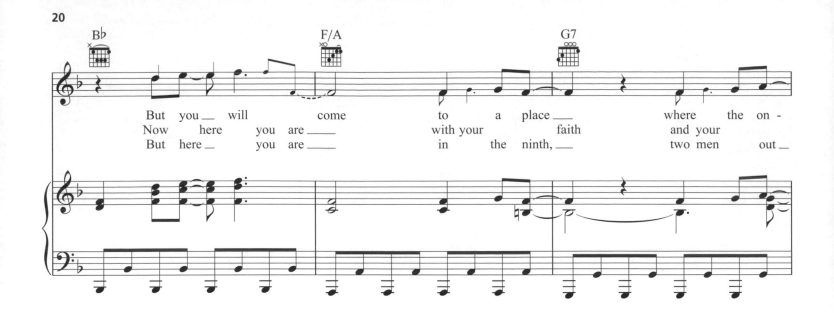

But you ___ will come to a place ___ where the on -
Now here you are ___ with your faith ___ and your
But here ___ you are ___ in the ninth, ___ two men out ___

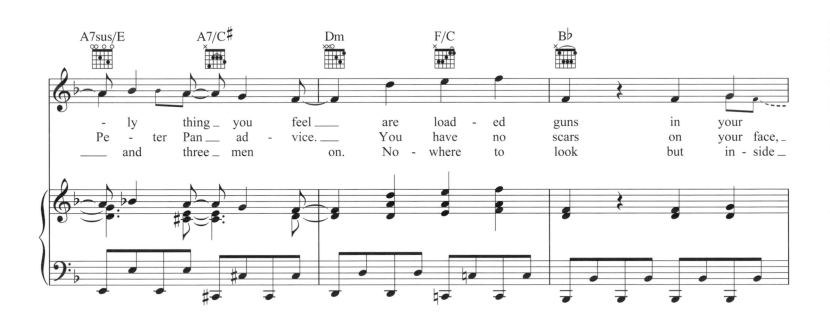

- ly thing ___ you feel ___ are load - ed guns in your
Pe - ter Pan ___ ad - vice. ___ You have no scars on your face,
___ and three ___ men on. No - where to look but in - side ___

face, and you'll have to deal ___ with pres - sure.
___ and you can - not han - dle
___ where we all ___ re - spond to

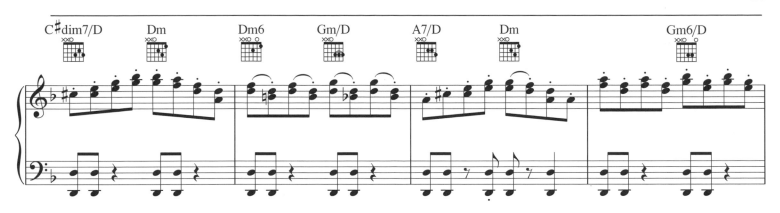

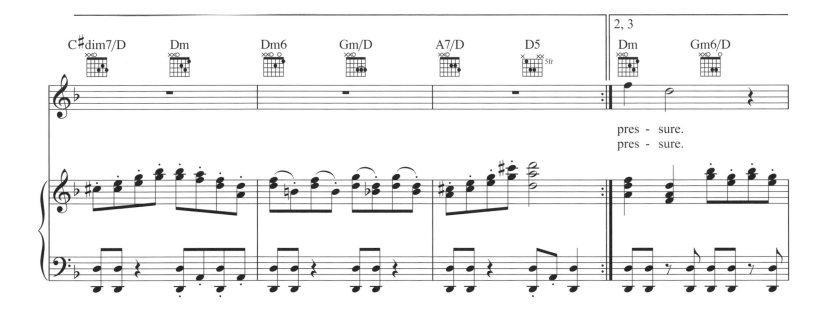

pres - sure.
pres - sure.

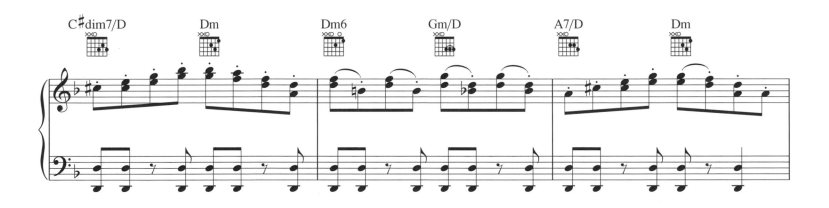

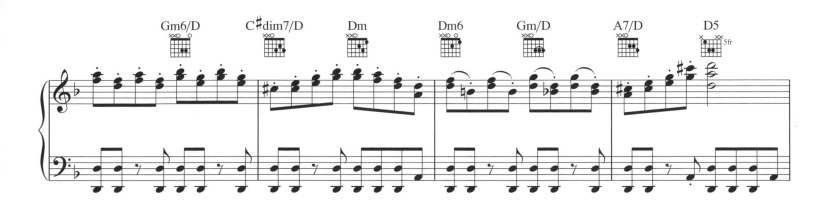

GOODNIGHT SAIGON

Words and Music by
BILLY JOEL

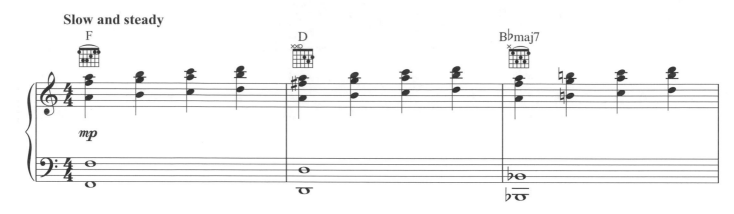

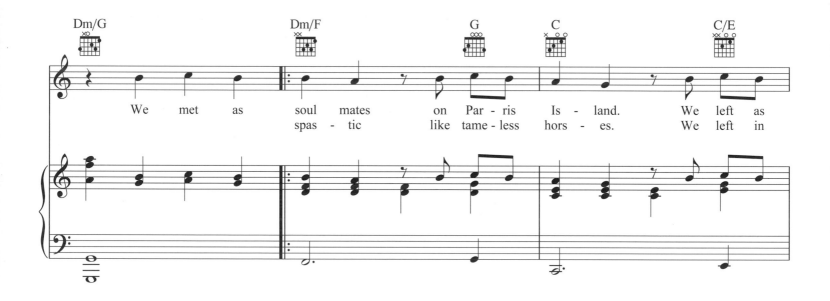

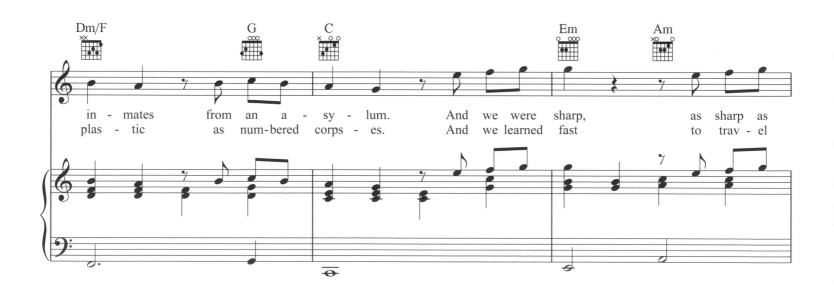

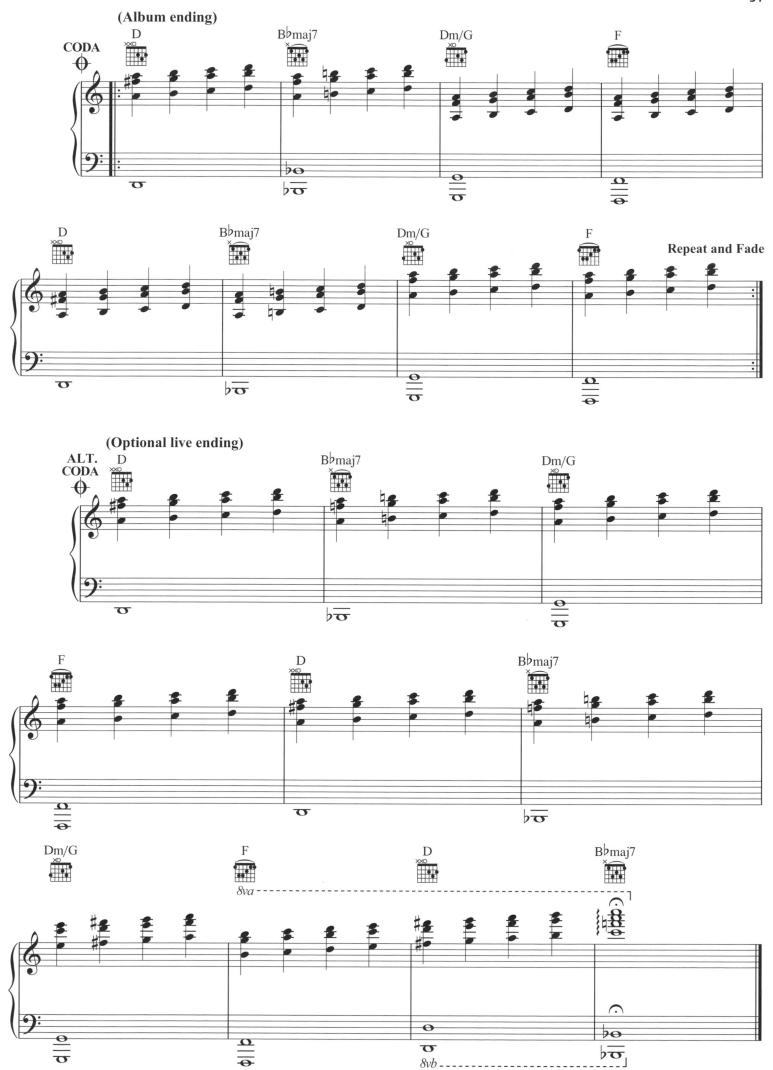

SHE'S RIGHT ON TIME

Words and Music by
BILLY JOEL

that should make _ the at - mos - phere com - plete. ___
soon she will _ be walk - ing through that door. ___

I've had to wait _ for - ev - er, but bet - ter late _ than nev - er. }
I may be go - ing no - where, but I ___ don't mind _ if she's _ there. }

She's just _ in time _ for me, ___ she's right _ on time, ___

She's just _ in time _ for me, ___ she's right _ on time, ___

Cmaj7   B   A7sus   A

Ev - 'ry time __ I lost __ the me - ter, there she was __ when I __ would need __ her,
Turn the cho - ral mu - sic high - er, pile more wood __ up - on __ the fi - re,

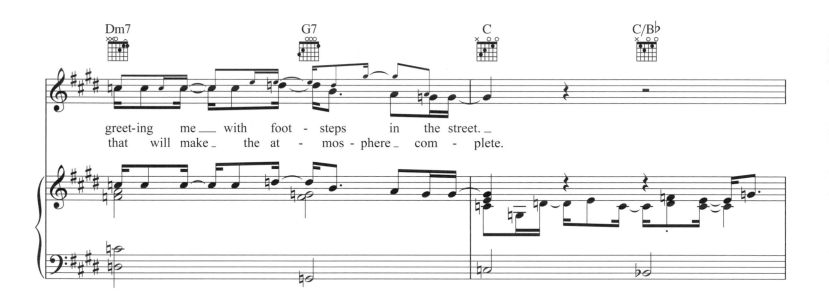

Dm7   G7   C   C/B♭

greet - ing me __ with foot - steps in the street. __
that will make __ the at - mos - phere __ com - plete.

F   G   Am   B(add4)

I guess I should __ have known __ it, she'd find __ the per - fect mo - ment.)
I've had to wait __ for - ev - er, but bet - ter late __ than nev - er.)

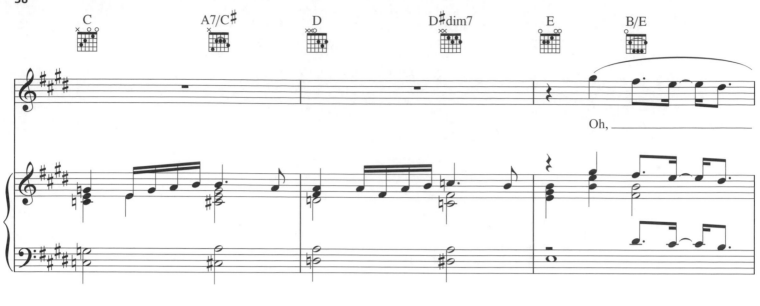

Oh, _____

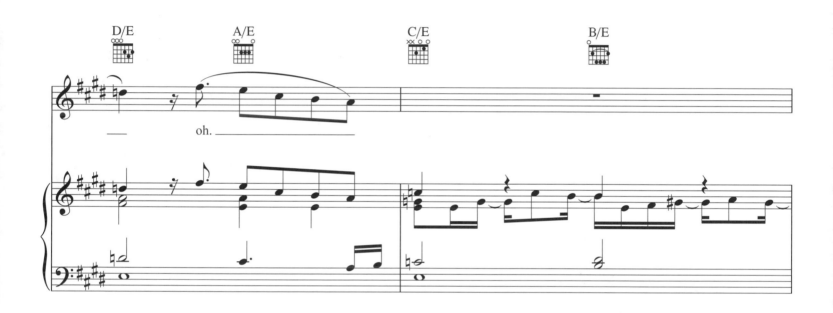

— oh. _____

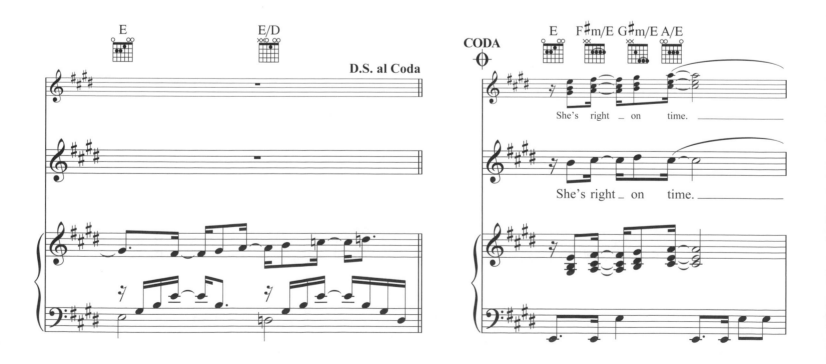

D.S. al Coda

CODA

She's right _ on time. _____

She's right _ on time. _____

A ROOM OF OUR OWN

Words and Music by
BILLY JOEL

Fast Rock, Swing

A7(no3)

A7(no3)   D7

You've _ got dia - monds _ and I've _ got spades.
You've _ got the day shift _ now I've _ got nights.

F7   C7

You've _ got pills and I've _ got ra - zor blades. _
We _ go wrong at times, _ but we've got rights. _

SURPRISES

Words and Music by
BILLY JOEL

Moderately slow

Don't get ex - cit - ed, don't say a word.

No - bod - y no - ticed, noth - ing was heard. It was com - mit - ted dis - crete - ly, it was

han - dled so neat - ly, and it should - n't sur - prise _ you at all, _____ you know. _

Don't look now, but you have changed. Your best friends would -n't tell you.

Now it's ap-par-rent, now it's a fact. __ So mar-shall your forc - es for an-

SCANDINAVIAN SKIES

Words and Music by
BILLY JOEL

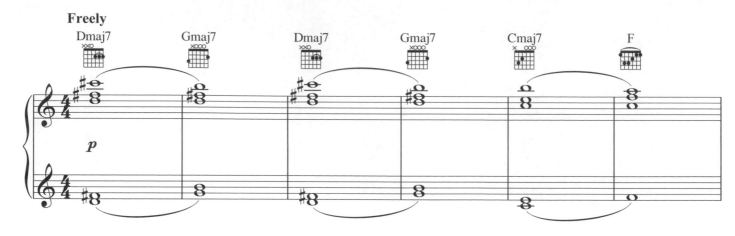

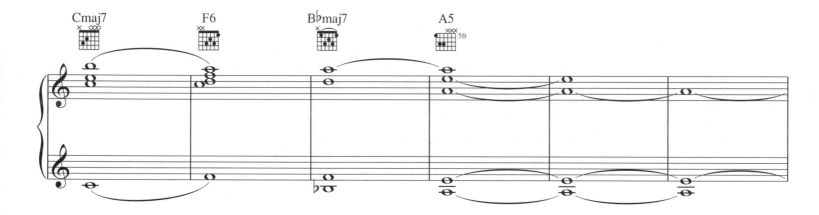

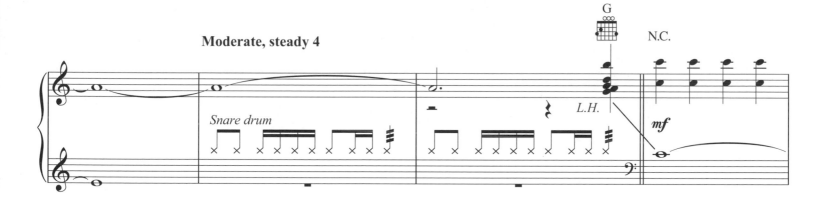

we turned and cursed __ as one, ____ we pulled the shades __

__ and closed __ our __ eyes, _____ eyes. _____

The Stock-holm
The tour of

cit - y lights __ were slow - ly start - ing to rise ____
Ger - ma - ny ___ was bleed - ing in - to our eyes ____

*See ossia on page 58.

WHERE'S THE ORCHESTRA?

Words and Music by
BILLY JOEL